LAWNS

KENNETH A. BECKETT

COLLINS

Products mentioned in this book

Benlate* + 'Activex'	contains	benomyl
'Clean-Up'	contains	tar acids
'Lawnsman' Mosskiller	contains	chloroxuron, dichlorophen ferrous sulphate
'Lawnsman' Weed & Feed	contains	dicamba/2,4–D
'Sybol'	contains	pirimiphos-methyl
'Verdone' 2	contains	2,4–D and mecoprop

Products marked thus '*Sybol*' are trade marks of Imperial Chemical Industries plc
*Benlate** is a registered trade mark of Du Pont's
Read the label before you buy: use pesticides safely.

Editor Emma Johnson
Designers James Marks, Steve Wilson
Picture research Moira McIlroy

This edition first published 1988 by
William Collins Sons & Co Ltd
London · Glasgow · Sydney
Auckland · Toronto · Johannesburg

© Marshall Cavendish Limited 1985, 1988

British Library Cataloguing in Publication Data

Beckett, Kenneth A.
    Lawns.——(Collins Aura garden handbooks).
    1. Lawns
    I. Title
    635.9′647   SB433

ISBN 0–00–412382–4

Photoset by Bookworm Typesetting
Printed and bound in Hong Kong by Dai Nippon Printing
Company

Front and back cover photographs by the
Harry Smith Horticultural Photographic Collection

CONTENTS

INTRODUCTION

A lawn of the right shape and size in the right place can do wonders for a garden, providing a splendid foil for the flowers and adding an air of peace and maturity to the house. Lawns also form an important recreation area for all sorts of children's and adults' games, barbecues and sunbathing. Despite these benefits, the lawn is probably the most maltreated area of the garden. We expect to weed, feed, water and generally care for the vegetables and flowers, but in most gardens the grass plants that form the lawn get none of this treatment. Mowing is the only regular attention that all lawns receive, and this is usually carried out as a chore equal to vacuuming the carpet.

Imagine what a row of cabbages or lettuces would look like after having all their leaves cut back by half once a week all through the growing season. Miserable little plants would result, especially if the soil had not been prepared or fed first. This analogy is not entirely apt, because grass plants have to be cut back regularly to form a sward, but the point being made is that to stay healthy and vigorous, even grass needs attention. Without the sort of yearly care outlined in this booklet, a lawn soon becomes weed-infested and is taken over by annual meadow grass and moss that quickly fade during a dry spell. A close look at most suburban lawns will show that this is usually the case.

Throughout the world some 10,000 different sorts of grasses are known, but very few are used to form lawns. Those that are must be able to stand frequent cutting and form the dense green covering that makes a good lawn. Just as the best brands of tea and coffee are blends, so the most satisfactory lawns are a mixture of several types of grass. The species used depends on the purpose to which the lawn is to be put, and this is dealt with more fully under the heading 'Seed mixtures' on pages 18-19.

The lawn has evolved from the mown hay meadows and, although highly artificial, is a plant community in its own right. Unless newly sown, hay meadow grasses vary in different parts of the country, and even the newly sown ones will soon be invaded by the grass species indigenous to the area. In a lesser way this happens to the garden lawn unless a rigorous routine of cultivation is followed. In the amenity lawn this matters little, but for a high quality ornamental lawn it should always be borne in mind.

A well-tended lawn is a valuable feature of any garden. The fine texture and colour of a healthy lawn enhances flower displays, trees and shrubs. In a more practical way, an expanse of grass, whatever the size, provides a play area for children and a peaceful place to sit in fine weather.

7

Shape and size The shape and size of a lawn is largely determined by that of the garden, although on the whole we are not adventurous enough to exploit the situation to the full. All too often a lawn is square or oblong when an irregular, curving shape would be more satisfactory and easier to mow. Sweeping curves lead the eye away into the distance and can create an illusion of greater spaciousness.

Generally, the larger the lawn the more effective it is, provided it is complemented and contrasted with well-planned and planted beds and borders. The larger lawn can be enhanced by a small specimen flowering tree or conifer, a clump of pampas grass or a bed of flowers, but the effect of a small lawn is lost if treated in this way and will look rather fussy.

The very small lawn, say less than 3m × 3m (10ft × 10ft), can look rather paltry, and where the garden is very small there is much to be said for either creating a paved area or using plants such as thyme or chamomile (see pages 10-11) instead of a traditional lawn.

Gardens are not always a standard shape and you can add character or disguise awkward shapes with paths, indentations or curved edges. A sweeping curve, for example, will create an illusion of space in a short wide garden (left) and ornamental trees or shrubs help to disguise a long narrow lawn (right).

ALTERNATIVES TO GRASS

Although it has long been the tradition to use grasses for lawns, there are other plants that will provide a smooth green ground covering. These are particularly useful in the very small garden where a tiny grass lawn looks out of place. Several of these plants are aromatic when walked upon and have a very pleasing texture.

Chamomile has had its devotees for centuries. It is a mat-forming plant with narrow ferny leaves and white daisy-like flowers. The best type to obtain is 'Treneague', which rarely flowers, so needs little or no mowing or clipping. Prepare the soil in the way recommended for grass (pages 12-15), but if it is clay or a sticky loam that stays wet in winter, fork coarse sand into the top few inches at the rate of a 4.5 litre bucket per sq.m (1 gal. per sq.yd) and finish off with a 2.5cm (1in) layer of sand. Place the plants 25-30cm (9-12in) apart each way and weed regularly until they touch.

Wild thyme (sold as *Thymus serpyllum* or *T. drucei*) also makes a pleasing aromatic lawn which only needs one annual trim after flowering.

Dutch clover Where the soil dries quickly and you have little desire for lawn maintenance, white or Dutch clover can make a rich green lawn that does not brown, even in the driest summer, once it is thoroughly established. Seeds can usually be obtained from an agricultural seedsman, although it may not be easy to buy small amounts. About 30g per sq.m (1oz per sq.yd) is sufficient. Rake the seed well into the soil surface. Mowing should be unnecessary in the first year, but thereafter it should be done once or twice after flowering.

A chamomile lawn (left and far left) is particularly good in small areas where the soil is dry and sandy. Like thyme, its fine aromatic leaves make it an attractive ground cover. Clover (below) provides an easy-to-manage, rich green cover, but it needs an alkaline soil to succeed.

PREPARING THE SITE

If a lawn is to be created from scratch, the following points will need to be considered and acted upon. The area chosen should, if possible, be open to the sky. At the very least it should not be shaded for more than half the day in summer. Grass will grow in shade, but special seed mixtures must be used to create a good sward. Even so, grass in shade is loose in texture and will not stand up to hard wear.

A lawn, once laid, is likely to remain for a lifetime, or at least for many years, so there is much to be said for giving it a good start. If the final top soil is very chalky or sandy, then it should be enriched during preparation. Once the site has been roughly levelled, and before treading and raking, apply a 2.5-5cm (1-2in) deep dressing of moss peat and fork into the top 10-15cm (4-6in) of soil. Well-decayed garden compost, manure or spent hops passed through a 1cm (½in) sieve may also be used.

Fertilizing On all but the richer soils, it is an advantage to apply a general fertilizer over the peat before forking in. Growmore fertilizer at 60-90g per sq.m (2-3oz per sq.yd) is recommended, or a proprietary lawn fertilizer, such as 'Lawnsman' Autumn Feed, used according to the maker's instructions.

If the site is level and well drained, then fork the surface to a depth of 10-15cm (4-6in), breaking down any lumps as fine as possible. The next stage is to add peat or fertilizer as recommended above, then tread firmly. Rake the whole area to a fine tilth to provide a good surface for sowing or turfing.

When to prepare This preparation can be done at almost any time of the year, providing that the soil is not wet and sticky. However, clay or sticky loam soils are best prepared in autumn and left rough after forking for the winter frosts to break down the lumps. During the first dry spell in late winter or early spring, rake the surface over, tread and rake again. Lighter soils are best prepared in summer for a late summer to early autumn sowing or turfing.

Weeds If possible it is always an advantage to prepare the soil several months before it is needed, there

On a well-drained site break down lumps with a fork and tread the soil firmly. Take short, overlapping steps, placing weight firmly on heels (1). Rake and re-rake the soil in different directions, removing any large stones or debris as you go (2). About a week before sowing or turfing, apply a fertilizer (3). Lightly rake it into the surface. Within a few months the new lawn may show signs of unevenness. Top-dressing with alternate layers of manure and sandy loam soil will improve the surface (4).

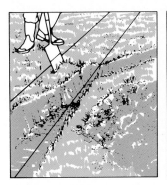 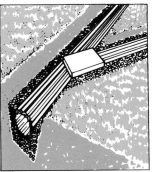 

Draining a site 1. Dig trenches about 45cm (1½ft) deep. Side trenches should meet main drain at 60° angle.

2. When the pipes and/or gravel is laid, cover junctions with a flat tile to prevent blockages.

3. If there is no watercourse, construct a soakaway 1.8m (6ft) deep. Line with bricks and fill with rubble.

will then be time for any weed seedlings or perennial weeds to show through and be dealt with by hoeing or application of a weedkiller such as 'Weedol'. There is less need to do this if turf is being used as this effectively prevents any annual weeds from germinating, and any perennial weeds that eventually push through are weakened and finally killed by regular mowing.

Wet sites If you are really unfortunate your chosen site may be very wet or even waterlogged. Fine grasses will not tolerate these conditions and the surface will be unpleasant to walk on. If this waterlogging occurs only during wet winters, it is best to avoid using the lawn until it dries out naturally in spring. If however, you have to walk on the lawn during winter, or if it stays wet for much of the year, then some sort of drainage system must be installed.

Drainage systems Drains are the most efficient – 5-7.5cm (2-3in) diameter earthenware pipes laid end to end across the site at a depth of about 30-45cm (1-1½ft) and with a gentle fall to a ditch or soakaway. For the less wet sites, coarse gravel, stone or clinker can be used instead of pipes, filling from about 30-45cm (1-1½ft) to about 15cm (6in) from the final level, then finishing up with 15cm (6in) of top soil, firmed well as it is put back.

A raised lawn It may be that there is no possible outlet for a drainage system. The only alternative in this case is to build a raised lawn by putting down 7.5-15cm (3-6in) of coarse gravel or stones and covering this with a minimum of 7.5cm (3in) of top soil.

Lawns on new sites All too often, a new garden site is fouled by builders' rubbish and this can mean a lot of extra hard work. The most obvious things, such as broken bricks, chunks of hardened cement and paint tins, must be removed.

However, often most damaging to a new lawn are the heaps of sub-soil, (clay, sand or pure chalk) which completely cover the original fertile top-soil. This is most likely to occur on sloping sites where the ground has been levelled by a bulldozer. If possible the sub-soil should be removed or mixed with the top-soil beneath by digging with a fork.

Where the site is very large or deeply covered with sub-soil it is best to bow to the inevitable and buy in top-soil to cover it up and provide a fertile medium for the grass. Before this is done, go over the intended lawn area, stabbing it with a fork to make sure that there are no large chunks of cement or other obstructions near the surface. If this is not done, the very thin soil layer which covers them will dry out too quickly and the grass will suffer during spells of drought.

Sloping lawns and terraces Ideally the surface of a lawn should be smooth, but it need not be horizontal. Indeed, where the site permits, a gently sloping lawn can be very

Terracing 1. Clear away any rubble left by builders, remove the top-soil and set to one side.

2. Rake the sub-soil down to the desired level. Stretch a line across to divide terrace into upper and lower section.

3. Transfer sub-soil from upper section to bring two halves level. Replace the top-soil, tread firmly and rake over.

A sloping lawn (right) is a very attractive feature of a large garden, although it does make mowing more difficult. Gardens with a very steep slope are best terraced (left) to make the area more manageable.

effective. A large lawn may even be undulating, but the contours must be gentle enough for the mower to negotiate them efficiently.

Steeply sloping gardens are best terraced to reduce the lawn slope to a more manageable pitch. If terracing is contemplated, the top-soil (the top 10-15cm (4-6in) is enough) must first be removed and set to one side. Next fork over the sub-soil, rake down to the desired levels and, once the terracing has been completed, tread firmly. Spread the top-soil back and tread again. If necessary you can build a retaining wall before you replace the top-soil and resume work on the next terrace. Finally rake to give a fine tilth.

By whatever hard or easy means the work is carried out, the ultimate result should be a smooth-surfaced site of fertile, well drained soil ready to bear a lawn.

SEED OR TURF?

Even before the site is prepared, some thought should be given to the way in which the lawn is to be started. There are two main alternatives – turf and seeds. If cost is no obstacle, or if an instant lawn is wanted, then turf it must be. If these considerations are set aside, however, then seeding must be considered to have more advantages. The following table sets out the merits of both methods.

Seeds (for)
1 Much cheaper.
2 Easy to lay (sow).
3 A grass mixture can be selected for a specific purpose, e.g. hard wearing, shade-tolerant or a high-quality, show lawn.
4 Seed can be bought in advance and sown when conditions are right.

Seeds (against)
1 Slow to produce a sward which can be used regularly.

Turf (for)
1 Once laid is soon established and can be used.

Turf (against)
1 Far more expensive; good quality turf is four times as dear as seed.
2 Not easy to lay well.
3 Most turf comes from old meadows and building sites and often contains unwanted coarse grasses and weeds.

Velvet bent grass There is a third alternative, using short pieces of the stems of velvet or creeping bent grass. These are spread evenly over the site and covered with a thin layer of soil. From then until they are rooted and growing well, they must not dry out or the result could be a total failure. In addition, this grass is shallow rooted and creeping, easily uprooted and prone to drought. Stem pieces for planting are often in limited supply. However, under ideal conditions of soil fertility and moisture, it can form a velvety, springy lawn of high visual appeal.

Seed mixes There are several grass seed mixtures available for specific purposes. These fall into three groups: hard-wearing, shade-tolerant and fine-leaved.

Unless you want a fine lawn, mainly for ornamental purposes, the hard wearing mixtures are best. All of these have perennial rye grass as the tough, strong-growing basic ingredient, plus Chewing's fescue and crested dogstail, sometimes also with a little rough-stalked meadow grass. You can make up a mixture of your own, but for small amounts it is not really practical and it is advisable to buy a ready-made and well-tested mixture from a reputable seedsman.

For those who really do want to make up their own, a recommended mixture is as follows: 4 parts perennial rye grass S23, 4 parts Chewing's fescue and 2 parts crested dogstail. If the area to be sown is shaded, a suitable mixture is 5 parts rough stalked meadow grass, 3 parts smooth stalked meadow grass and 2 parts creeping red fescue.

There are a number of good proprietary fine lawn mixtures, all of which should contain mainly Chewing's fescue with a little brown top bent. A recommended mixture would be these two in a ratio of 8 to 2. Beware of cheap so-called 'fine lawn' mixtures as quite often they contain both crested dogstail and perennial rye grasses, which soon take over the fine grasses unless very carefully tended and close mown.

Different types of lawn grasses are suited to different types of soil, but most seedsmen supply good proprietary mixes, suitable in a wide range of conditions.

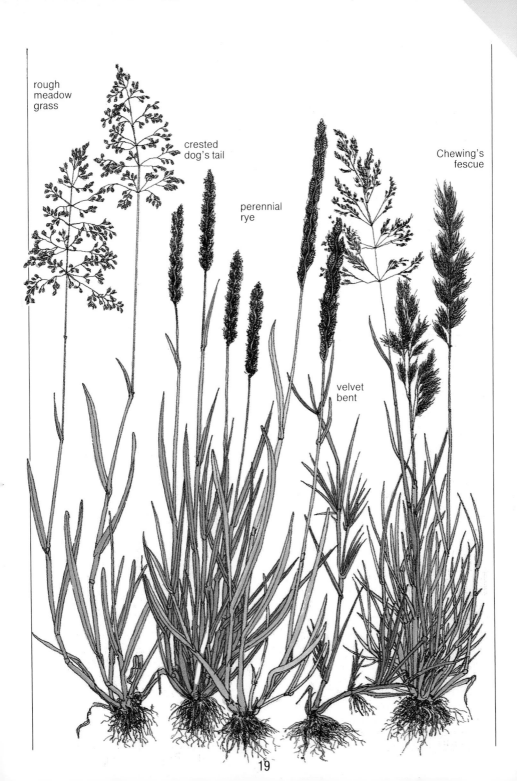

rough
meadow
grass

crested
dog's tail

perennial
rye

Chewing's
fescue

velvet
bent

19

SOWING

Grass seed can be sown at almost any time of the year except winter, but the optimum times are late summer to early autumn and spring. Autumn is probably the best time as one can expect enough rain to keep the soil moist, and there are enough wild seeds around to prevent an invasion of sparrows or other seed-eating birds. In the northern parts of the country where autumn is often cool and wet, a spring sowing is recommended, but in the south, particularly the south-east, spring can be very dry and some form of irrigation might be needed.

Grass seeds vary from small to very small and all are extremely light. Ideally, therefore, a fairly windless day should be chosen. Make sure that the soil is moist, although the extreme surface can be dry when the seeds are raked in.

How thickly to sow The aim is to sow seed thick enough to achieve a good grass cover as soon as possible to compete with the weeds. On the other hand, too thick a sowing can result in the seedlings damping off and succumbing to diseases. If the soil is fertile, and has been weeded several times before sowing, 30g per sq.m (1oz per sq.yd) is adequate. On the poorer, weedier soils, as much as 90g (3oz) may be needed. For average garden conditions, 60g (2oz) is recommended to give a good crop of seedlings.

How to sow Sowing large areas is best done with a sowing machine, or broadcast with a forwards sweeping motion of the hand like the old method of sowing grain crops. Mark out the lawn area with strings 1m (3ft) apart. Weigh out several 30g (1oz) lots (or whatever seeding rate is chosen), then take a rod or cane at least 1m (3ft) long to mark off a square metre at the beginning of one of the strips. Sprinkle the seeds as evenly as possible, then mark off the next metre and so on. When the entire lawn has been sown, gently rake the surface with long steady strokes of the rake. Some of the seeds will still show after raking, but enough will be covered, and even those on the surface will germinate if the soil is moist enough.

Lawn strips For those who do not want the bother of sowing, or who doubt their ability to do it well, lawn strips are available. These look like rolls of paper and have the seed imbedded in the surface. After preparing the soil, the strips are unrolled, cut to size and anchored with a thin layer of soil. This method is more expensive than straightforward seeding, but is probably worthwhile for a small lawn.

Protecting the seed Where birds are known to be troublesome, either by eating the seeds or dust-bathing in the dry soil, some form of protection will be needed. Several proprietary seed mixtures are treated with non-poisonous bird deterrents, but these cannot be relied upon to give full protection. Light, twiggy sticks can be laid across the newly sown area until germination starts, or the time-honoured black cotton stretched on sticks. Use pure cotton as nylon, or thread strengthened with nylon, does not break easily and can trap birds if it becomes twisted around their legs.

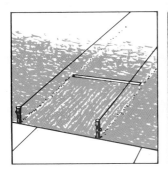

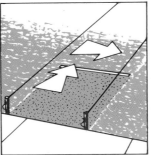

1. Mark out the lawn area with strings 1m (3ft) apart to create strips.

2. Sow in both directions, as indicated, to achieve an even coverage of seed.

3. Rake the surface lightly. Apply a light top-dressing (below) a couple of months after seeds have germinated.

Maintaining a new lawn When the seedlings are 2.5-4cm (1-1½in) tall, it is a good idea to give the lawn a light rolling. This helps to firm the little plants and encourages tillering (branching from the base). A few days after the grass has been rolled, give the new lawn a light mowing. Set the machine to 2.5cm (1in) and make sure that the blades are both sharp and well set. Mow regularly at this height for the first few months, then if it is to be a high-quality ornamental lawn, lower the blades to the correct setting (see mowing section pages 28-29).

During this early period, broad-leaved weeds can be a nuisance. It is best not to use weedkillers while the grass is so small and weeds should be removed by hand. Divide the area into 1m (1yd) wide strips and work down each one with a widger or old kitchen knife and remove all weeds. Watch out for coarse, broad-leaved grasses if the mixture is a fine one and remove these as well.

During dry spells irrigation or watering of some sort must be carried out if the grass is to grow rapidly and knit together.

About two months after germina-tion, or the spring following an autumn sowing, a light top-dressing of good soil can be applied to advantage. Ideally, this should be a reliable soil-based potting compost such as one of the John Innes, but good garden soil mixed with equal parts of peat and sand, passed through a 0.6cm (¼in) sieve is equally effective. The layer should be about 1-2.5cm (½-1in) deep and worked into the grass plants with the back of a rake, applying more to level out any depressions. If the grass is growing slowly, especially after a hard winter, apply some lawn tonic at the same time. This is also a good time to resow any bare areas.

TURFING

Turf used for lawns has varied origins, but it can be roughly classified into three groups: the first is natural meadow or hillside grassland, often stripped when foundations for new housing estates are prepared; the second covers grass of similar origin, but kept short and treated with weedkillers to remove most of the major weeds; and the third is grass purposefully sown and tended as a lawn.

Most of the cheapest, easily available turf falls into the first group. As long as it is not too weedy, it provides the basis for a good, hard-wearing lawn. However, it must be fed, treated with weedkiller and mowed regularly.

The second group looks better on laying, but it is expensive and is probably not worth buying unless it is only marginally dearer than group one turf. Also in this group is the very fine-leaved Cumberland or sea marsh turf. This is largely used for bowling greens and lawns of the highest quality. It needs very well-drained soil and special care, and is not recommended for the average garden.

The third group provides the best quality turf, but it is more expensive than the others and is usually more difficult to obtain. It will only be better than groups one and two if it has been well-tended and, unless the vendor will specify the type of grasses it contains, there is little point in paying the usually very high price. What turf chiefly provides is the instant lawn and all groups (except the specialist Cumberland) will respond to routine treatment and form a good lawn in time.

Turf is often cut mechanically on a large scale and is then of a uniform thickness, usually about 2.5-4cm (1-1½in). Whether cut by hand or machine it will be lifted in strips 1m × 30cm (3 × 1ft), so it is easy to work out how many turves will be needed for a lawn of a known size. Unless the turves are to be laid within 24 hours of delivery, it is best to lay them out flat and keep them just moist until the site is ready for laying. If turves are stacked for more than a few days, the leaves will turn yellow and the stack may heat up in the middle, killing both leaves and roots. Ideally, turves should be laid within a week of delivery.

When to turf Ideally turfing should be carried out in autumn, or late winter to early spring when new roots will form and grow vigorously. However it can be done at almost any time of the year, except when the soil is frozen or there are drought conditions. Soil preparation is the same as for sowing seed, although it is not necessary to rake the surface to such a fine tilth. If possible, prepare the soil a week or more before laying and apply a dressing of general lawn fertilizer, e.g. 'Lawnsman' Autumn Feed, according to manufacturer's instructions.

Make sure that the turves are of uniform thickness. Sometimes hand-cut turves vary and this can upset the final levels. If only a few turves are extra thick, it is usually possible to skim off some of the soil and roots with a sharp spade. If many are thick, it will be necessary to box them. A turf box should have internal measurements of 1m × 30cm (3 × 1ft) and one end can be open to slide the turf in. The depth should be

Laying turf
Press the first row of turves into position. Place a plank over them and lay the second row, staggering them like bricks (1). Roll the turf in one direction, then in the other to smooth it down (2). Brush the lawn to lift the flattened surface of the grass (3). Finally, use a half-moon turf cutter to trim the edges (4).

that of the average turf supplied, usually 2.5-4cm (1-1½in). Place the turf upside down in the box and run a sharp spade or a proper two hand-led turfing knife along the edges of the box, removing all soil and roots that rise above it.

All this assumes that the lawn is square or rectangular in outline. If it is curved, round or oval, start by marking the outline and laying the first row of turves around this. Each turf will bend slightly sideways, but to get them to end satisfactorily it is usually necessary to slice a small wedge-shaped piece from the end. The final turves in the centre will probably have to be cut to fit.

If the lawn is a very small circle or oval it may be best to lay the turves in a straight line across it, trimming to shape afterwards. Mark out curved edges and cut with a half-moon turfing tool.

In addition to providing a path-way over the prepared, raked soil, the use of a plank will firm the turves after laying. Any that miss the plank should be tapped down with the flat back of a spade. A light rolling can be done, but should not be necessary. If there are any cracks between turves after laying, these should be filled. Use a mixture of peat and sand, working into the surface with the back of a rake.

After care It is essential that newly laid turf does not dry out, and watering must be done regularly if drought conditions prevail. Autumn-laid turf will not need mowing until the following spring, but a spring-laid lawn will need its first cut about three to four weeks after laying. The grass must be given time to grow properly, to make leaf and root, so do not mow too closely while it is establishing itself. The first cut should only be a light 'topping'; then lower the blades on the mower in subsequent cuts.

RENOVATING A NEGLECTED LAWN

On moving into a new property one may be faced with a lawn that has been neglected and looks weedy and unkempt. If the lawn is taken over between spring and autumn the first thing to do is to mow it, setting the blades high, at 1.5-2.5cm (¾-1in), so that they do not get fouled by over-thick grass.

After mowing, work the lawn over with a wire tined rake to remove dead grass bases and moss, then mow again at 1.2cm (½in) setting. Apply a proprietary lawn fertilizer and, if the weather is dry, water it in. As soon as the grass is growing well, mow again. If there are a lot of broad-leaved weeds dig out the thickest patches and apply a weed-killer, such as 'Verdone' 2 to the rest. If there are any bare areas, loosen the surface with a fork, smooth over with a rake and sow with fresh seed. Alternatively dig out the bare area and lay pieces or plugs of turf.

If the lawn is taken over during the winter the initial mowing with the blades set high can still be carried out, but wait for a mild spell. Raking and hand weeding can follow, but again wait for mild spells. Only when spring arrives is it time to apply fertilizer and weedkiller. Thereafter, routine mowing, feeding and watering will ensure a worthwhile lawn.

A lawn from rough or neglected grass A new house may have part of an original grass field that is in the right place for a lawn. If it is level and not too infested with weeds or coarse, broad-leaved grasses, then

Renovating a lawn
The first step is to clear away excessive growth and then mow the area, setting the mower blades high. Follow this by raking, preferably with a spring-tined rake (right). Rake thoroughly to remove surface debris, straggly grasses and weeds. Then mow again, at right angles to the direction of raking.

1. Old lawns may be uneven. Level the site by digging up top-soil and putting it aside.

2. Even out the sub-soil, filling any hollows. Then replace the top-soil.

A neglected lawn will need food. Distribute a lawn fertiliser (below) over the surface.

4. Use the back of a wooden rake to distribute top-dressing evenly.

3. Apply top-dressing with a shovel (about 4lb per sq yd).

there is every chance of turning it into a very serviceable lawn.

The method of working depends upon the time of year. If starting in late autumn to spring, first work it over carefully, removing dead seeding stems with rake and shears. Dig out any large weeds that are clearly visible along with tussock-forming, broad-leaved grasses such as cocksfoot and apply weedkiller before growth hardens. Fill any holes or depressions ready for seeding in spring.

If starting during the spring to autumn period, the first task will be reducing the length of the grass to a manageable size. Unless the grass is very thick this can be done with a rotary motor mower or auto-scythe, scythette or shears. Aim to cut back to about 5cm (2in) high, then go over the surface as already described, finishing off with a dressing of 'Lawnsman' Lawn Feed fertilizer or Growmore at 60g per sq.m (2oz per sq.yd). Any depressions can be sown immediately they are filled. Now go over the area with a lawnmower at its highest possible setting. Make the next mowing at the same height, but thereafter reduce to 0.75cm (¾in). From now on follow the maintenance recommendations on pages 26-41.

LAWN MAINTENANCE

All too often a newly laid lawn is allowed to degenerate. In some respects a lawn is like a car – with regular servicing and maintenance you can keep it in good condition and avoid having to take drastic and remedial action. Simply mowing a lawn is not enough. Yearly feeding, liming, watering and aerating are all necessary if you want to keep it in fine condition.

MOWERS AND MOWING

Mowing is the one essential operation that turns an area of grass into a lawn. As grass leaves elongate from the base they will stand frequent amputation of their tips. This pruning also helps to create the dense basal growth essential for a thick-piled lawn.

Mowing not only keeps the grass short and neat, it also affects the composition of the grass and weed species involved. Annual weeds such as groundsel are soon killed out by regular mowing and many perennial weeds, such as bindweed and gout-weed (ground elder), are killed out in two to three years by regular cutting. Broad-leaved tufted gras-ses, such as cocksfoot, are also weakened to the point of extinction, but are best finally dug out.

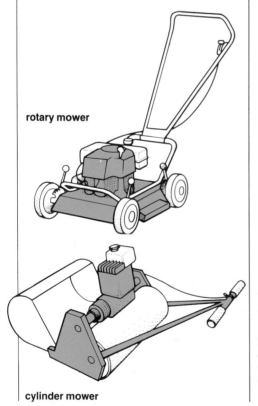

rotary mower

cylinder mower

Generally, the finer leaved the grass, the closer it can be mowed. High-quality ornamental lawns, mainly of fescues, can be cut to a height of 1cm (½in) and at such heights most weeds are eliminated. The coarser grasses, such as peren-nial rye, which make up the hard-wearing lawns, should be cut at about 2-2.5cm (¾-1in). Lower than this will weaken the grasses and allow such weed grasses as annual meadow grass to creep in.

When to mow Mowing should be carried out regularly. If the grass is allowed to get too long and is then cut hard, subsequent grass will be coarse and pale, particularly in spring and summer. This sort of treatment also tends to create a more open grass mat, allowing such weeds as creeping buttercup, dande-lions and clover to become estab-lished. Aim to mow each time before the grass blades reach twice the height of the optimum cut; for exam-ple, hard-wearing lawns at 2cm (¾in) high should not exceed 3.5cm (1½in) before mowing – 2.5-3cm (1-1¼in) would be ideal.

If mowing is done regularly in this way the pieces of grass blade will be small and there is no need to use a box on the mower. The fine mowings will be distributed over the surface of the lawn and lost to sight, soon to rot and form a useful mulch. Howev-er, if the mowings are longer or thicker and lie in windrows or clots they should be raked up and re-move before they begin to stifle the grass beneath them.

Patterns of mowing It is usual to mow in continuous parallel strips up and down or across the lawn. If a cylinder machine with a roller is used this will create the pale and dark striping effect beloved of many lawn enthusiasts. It is advisable to mow in alternate directions at each mowing, up and down followed by across and back.

Mowers There are many different mowing machines available, both powered and hand-operated, designed to cut the smallest and largest lawns. These can be classified into two groups according to the method of cutting. Cylinder machines have a ring of blades set around a central spindle. This revolves when the machine is pushed or the motor started, bringing each blade in turn across a fixed plate. A scissor-like action is created as each blade crosses the plate and grass trapped between the two is severed cleanly. This type of machine gives the neatest and closest finish and is recommended for the quality ornamental lawn. It should only be used when the grass is dry and the ground moderately firm.

Rotary machines have propeller-like blades set horizontally which revolve at high speed, cutting the grass as much by their speed as their sharpness. Rotary machines which are usually power operated are best suited to the hard-wearing lawn or rough banks, where they will also deal very efficiently with grass allowed to grow too long.

If the surface is undulating, then a Flymo-type rotary machine which works on the hovercraft principle is to be recommended. This type of machine is also useful for cutting the grass when it is wet.

Whether the mower is power or hand-operated, rotary or cylinder, it must be maintained in good order. Hand-operated mowers must be regularly oiled and the blades sharpened. Motorised machines must be serviced regularly. If the mower is not working well then do not expect to have a lawn worthy of admiration.

Along with the all-essential mower, there are several other tools necessary to the proper maintenance of a lawn. Not all are essential, but they will invariably help you to create a neat and attractive lawn.

Edging and trimmers Even an otherwise scruffy lawn can look acceptable if it is mowed and neatly edged. Grass continually grows sideways from the edge of a lawn and soon looks untidy. For a small lawn, edging shears are the answer. These work on the same principle as hand shears, but have long handles set at right angles to the blades. Choose a pair which enable you to stand with a reasonably straight back to make for comfortable working.

Trimmers For the larger lawn a power-driven trimmer is a worth-while investment, but make sure there is plenty of clearance between the lawn edge and border soil.

Where grass comes close to a tree trunk, wall or fence, one of the nylon cord strimmers is indispensable, eliminating the chore of hand clipping those ragged tufts of grass stems that the mower leaves.

Essential lawn tools (below): garden spade and fork, rake and spring-tine rake for removing decaying growth, and a half-moon cutter for cutting turf and reshaping edges. Hand shears or trimmers are invaluable for giving the lawn a well-groomed look (right).

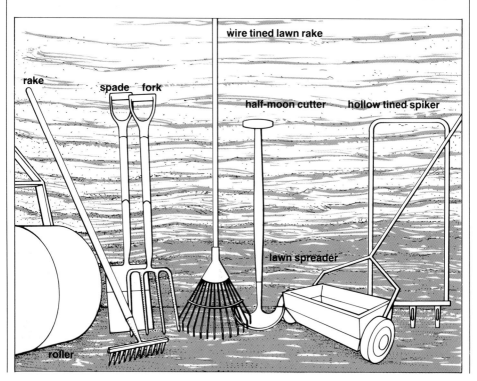

wire tined lawn rake

rake

spade fork

half-moon cutter   hollow tined spiker

lawn spreader

roller

Hand shears Although more sophisticated tools for trimming are now widely available, hand shears still have their use – particularly where a lawn area is very small. Make sure the handles have plenty of clearance when the blades are closed. Ideally, try several designs to make sure you have one that feels comfortable. If you have back troubles there are long-handled versions that do away with bending.

Leaf sweeps If the lawn is near trees the grass in autumn soon gets covered with a stifling blanket of fallen leaves. The usual method of removal is with a birch broom or a wood or plastic-toothed rake. However, large lawn areas can make this a real chore and a mechanical sweeper is worthwhile. Some rotary mowers with a grass catcher can be set high and used as leaf sweepers.

FEEDING AND LIMING

Although the average layman gardener accepts the fact that vegetable, fruit and flower plants must be fed from time to time, very few bother to feed their lawn. A lawn is a highly artificial thing, the grass plants being continually mutilated to keep them dwarf.

Leaves are the factories of all green plants, creating sugars and starches from carbon dioxide and oxygen via the energy of sunlight (photosynthesis). Continual removal of foliage from a lawn, therefore, weakens the grass plants, particularly if the mowings are raked off and not allowed to decay. There are comparable examples in the vegetable garden: for example, if rhubarb or spinach plants are over-picked they will subsequently produce smaller and poorer sticks or leaves, unless the soil is rich and moist.

To get the best and richest green Lawn it is essential to carry out an annual feeding programme. This need only be an annual application of a proprietary lawn fertilizer, such as 'Lawnsman' Lawn Feed. Do this in spring, just after the first mowing of the season, and then apply 'Lawnsman' Autumn Feed in autumn if the soil is poor and sandy or if the lawn has suffered drought conditions in summer.

For those who want to make up their own lawn feed, the following can be recommended: 2 parts sulphate of ammonia, 1 part hoof and horn meal or dried blood, 1 part

You can buy a simple kit (left) from any garden shop to test the pH level of soil. Take a sample from beneath the grass roots.

steamed bone flour, 1 part sulphate of potash and 4 parts of superphosphate. This must be applied evenly at 60-90g per sq.m (2-3oz per sq.yd), the larger amount on the poorer soils. To ensure an even distribution and to add extra organic matter to the soil, add 390-420g (13-14oz) of dryish soil or equal parts moss peat and soil, passed through a 0.6cm (¼in) sieve to every 60-90g (2-3oz) of the mixture. Each pound of mixture should then be spread over a square metre of lawn. On the richer, moister soils, and on lawns which have most of the mowings left *in situ*, the fertilizer mixture can be added to dry sand.

Lime and liming Although most of the fine-leaved fescue and bent grasses thrive on acid soils, growth tends to be poorer when acidity is very high. This can occur on soils reclaimed from heaths and moorlands and where the fertilizer sulphate of ammonia is used regularly over a number of years. To ascertain the degree of acidity the soil must be tested. This is easily done with one of the small kits that can be obtained from horticultural sundriesmen or garden centres.

The degree of acidity is measured in units of pH, based upon the amount of hydrogen ions it contains. A pH of 6.5-7 is neutral; below this level acidity increases, above it alkalinity increases. Soil samples should be taken from just beneath the grass roots and, if the test shows pH6 or less, a dressing of lime should be given, preferably in the form of ground chalk or limestone, during autumn.

Repeat this liming annually as rain and water soon leach it down below the grass roots into the subsoil. Do not exceed these recommendations as the breeding of earthworms is encouraged and many lawn weeds are more vigorous on limy soil.

Lime dressing

The amount per square metre of lime depends on the degree of acidity

pH6 – 60g (2oz)	pH4.5 – 240g (8oz)
pH5.5 – 120g (4oz)	pH4 – 300g (10oz)
pH5 – 180g (6oz)	

It is very rare that soil activity below pH4 occurs, but if it does, add 60g lime per sq.m (2oz sq.yd) for each 0.5 degree of pH.

Lawn spreaders are used to spread the fertiliser evenly over the grass. There are two kinds: the wheeled machine (far left) which can be bought or hired, and the fertiliser applicator (left) which shakes out a prescribed quantity and is good for small areas.

WATERING AND AERATING

With the exception of velvet bent, all the main lawn grasses in Britain are remarkably drought-resistant. However, to maintain a green sward of good texture the lawn should never lack adequate moisture during the main spring-to-autumn growing period. This means that on light, well-drained soils watering should start if no appreciative rain falls for two to three weeks at a time; on the heavier clay-type soils this period can be four to six weeks.

Watering should be thorough, sufficient being applied at one time to penetrate at least 15cm (6in) down into the soil. One good watering of this kind should last 7-10 days, depending on the amount of warm, sunny or windy weather.

Water should be applied gently and in as natural a way as possible to prevent flooding and compacting of the lawn surface. A watering-can with a rose is suitable for a very small lawn, but a hose and sprinkler is much better. There are many types of lawn sprinklers on the market and all are satisfactory under ideal conditions. Make sure that whatever system is chosen it adequately covers the lawn area. Try to avoid watering or irrigating with a sprinkler system during gusty windy weather when spray may be blown to one side of the lawn or even over onto a neighbour's flower border.

Aeration All roots need air if the plant they feed is to thrive, and grass is no exception. Lawns that have plenty of foot traffic suffer compac-

Aeration is the process of spiking the lawn to allow a free passage of air through the soil. This will help the grass root system. Few lawns need complete aeration, but some parts need attention. Small areas of lawn can be aerated with a garden fork. Penetrate the soil vertically by pushing the fork backwards into the turf, then ease it back and forth gently before removing.

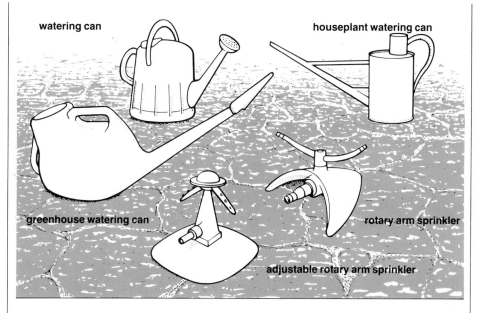

watering can

houseplant watering can

greenhouse watering can

rotary arm sprinkler

adjustable rotary arm sprinkler

tion of the soil surface by the autumn of each year and even the quality ornamental lawn will have similar but less severe troubles from being continually mowed, often with a roller attached.

This compaction of the soil surface slows the movement of oxygen down between the soil particles. Worms and soil insects help to break up this hard surface if given sufficient time, but these creatures are not desirable on lawns because of the nuisance they cause in other ways. (See Pests and Diseases pages 42-45.)

There are, however, several time-honoured mechanical means for aerating the surface. For a lawn on lighter, sandy soils scarifying with a wire rake is often enough. This tool has a fan-shaped arrangement of highly tempered steel wire teeth and is drawn firmly across the lawn surface so that the points of the teeth get down to the base of the grass roots. Apart from scratching the soil surface the main value of the wire rake is to loosen and remove

choking remains of dead grass and moss and prepare the lawn for a dressing of fertilizer. After this raking, a mowing is advantageous to remove the dragged-up grass stems.

For deeper aeration an ordinary digging fork should be used. Move up and down the lawn in strips, thrusting the fork straight in and out 10-15cm (4-6in) deep and the same number of inches apart. Spiked rollers are available for the larger lawn, but they are not particularly successful on the heavier clay-type soils. For these heavier soils it is best to use a hollow tined fork. This removes narrow cores from the lawn and thus does not make compacted holes in the way a solid tined fork does.

Once the lawn has been hollow-tined and spiked, brush off the cores of soil and apply a 50/50 peat and sand dressing, brushing this across the lawn so that it goes into the holes. About 4.6 litres (1 gallon) of peat and sand mix per square metre should be sufficient.

GENERAL MAINTENANCE

Feeding, watering and aeration of a lawn are tasks to be completed every year. Among lesser maintenance chores are removing bumps and hollows, trimming and repairing broken edges, and weeding.

Filling holes Unless hollows are more than 2.5cm (1in) deep they are easily dealt with by filling in with equal parts sand and soil or peat sand and soil passed through a 2cm (¾in) sieve. Start by putting down a few handfuls of this mixture and brushing or raking it well down in among the grass plants, then top up with more. Do not tread afterwards, but allow rain or watering to do the firming. Afterwards it may be necessary to top up with a little mixture.

Holes deeper than 2.5cm (1in) can either be filled in gradually by the above method, allowing the grass to grow up through the top dressing mixture, or the turf covering the depressed area can be lifted, a few handfuls of soil spread out and the turf replaced and firmed.

Levelling bumps Bumps are dealt with in the following way: take a sharp spade or half-moon turf cutter and cut a cross into the bump. Carefully fold back the four flaps of turf, scrape out the surplus soil forming the lump, then replace and firm the flaps.

Edging Even when regularly cut with edging shears the margins of the lawn can slowly encroach on the adjacent flower border, though it may be several years before it is noticeable. It should therefore be trimmed back to its original contour with a sharp half-moon cutter or spade. To make a neat and accurate job on a straight-edged lawn, first mark out the new boundary with a garden line.

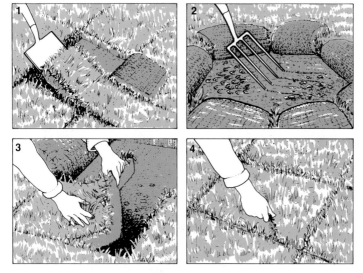

Levelling
Cut a cross over the middle of the bump, then cut parallel lines across to divide the area into rectangles of turf. Lift the turves at one end with a spade and fold them back (1). Scrape the soil with a fork to level the bump, and rake over (2). Replace the turves back and firm them down in position (3). Sprinkle fine soil in the cracks between the turves (4).

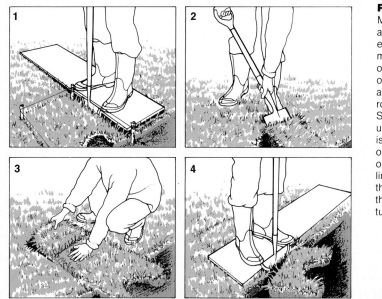

Repairing edges

Mark out a square around the broken edge and use a half-moon cutter to cut it out (1). Lift the piece of turf with a spade and pull it free of the roots and soil (2). Slide the turf forwards until the broken edge is beyond the border of the lawn. (3). Stand on a plank of wood, lined with the edge of the lawn and cut off the damaged piece of turf.

A half-moon turf cutter is an invaluable lawn tool. It is more precise than a spade and is used for cutting turf and reshaping or straightening the edges of the lawn. When repairing broken edges or pieces of turf, line up a plank of wood, hold it firm and cut along the edge with the half-moon tool (right).

Frequently the well-used lawn suffers a broken down area along one of its margins. To repair this, cut out an oblong or square area of turf at least 7.5cm (3in) all round the damaged area. Lift the piece of turf with a spade and push it forwards so that the broken edge is outside the border of the lawn, now facing outside. Firm in position, then fill in the gap with fresh soil and sow with a pinch or two of grass seeds. Alternatively, if there is some spare turf nearby use it to plug the damaged area.

WEEDS AND WEEDING

If you start with a comparatively weed-free seed bed or prepared turf that has few or no weeds, then attention to feeding, cutting at the right time and watering should ensure that weeds are only a minimal problem. This, however, is a counsel of perfection and in reality very few if any lawns are without some weeds.

Although the gardener now has a veritable battery of selective or hormone weed killers at his command, there is still no panacea that will remove all lawn weeds at one blow. If a wide range of weed species is present, then a hormone weedkiller such as 'Verdone' 2 will give good results if used in spring and summer. This will not deal with every lawn weed, but what remains may be hand weeded.

Some of the long-standing methods, such as raking the creeping weeds with a wire rake and mowing off the loosened portions and applying lawn sand, are still very effective if carried out regularly. Lawn sand is a mixture of sulphate of iron, sulphate of ammonia and sand and it has a corrosive effect on the broad leaves of dandelions, plaintains, daisies, and on dense patches of pearlwort and moss. To prevent any damage to the grass it is best used during showery weather or watered not later than two days after application. A well-tried formula is 1 part calcined sulphate of iron, 3 parts sulphate of ammonia mixed with 20 parts dry sand or finely sieved soil. The sulphate of ammonia also gives the grass a nitrogen feed, encouraging quick vigorous growth to fill in patches where the weeds have died. If large areas of weeds are removed by weedkillers of any type it is important to sow seeds or fill with a plug of turf to prevent recolonization by weed seedlings.

A well-cultivated lawn should be weed-free, but very few gardens are without any weeds. Cultural treatment of weeds – regular cutting, raking, feeding and watering – should prevent the spread of weeds such as Greater Plantain (below). Nowadays there are many lawn weedkillers available and these can be applied using sprays, cans, spot applicators or from a sprinkle bar on a watering can (below right).

Annual meadow grass This small, moderately broad-leaved grass is the saving grace of so many lawns that it is difficult to call it an outright weed. Nevertheless, its short-lived nature and proneness to drought make it an undesirable lawn grass and efforts should be made to eliminate it. Annual meadow grass is commonest on the poorer, lighter soils and on poorly maintained lawns regularly cut too short. It is very adaptable, spreading sideways to avoid the mower blades and capable of flowering and seeding under the most unpromising of conditions. It is also the commonest grass weed in the vegetable and flower borders for this same reason. Being a grass, it does not succumb to lawn weedkillers, but is easily squeezed out by regularly feeding the lawn and not cutting it too low.

Clover This covers the common red and white clover and several much smaller species known as trefoils, mainly with yellow flowers. All have leaves composed of three oval leaflets and they are not easily distinguished by the novice.

White clover is comparatively easy to control with hormone weedkillers, but other clovers are more resistant and require regular applications of a weedkiller such as 'Verdone' 2. Frequent use of lawn sand combined with wire raking and regular mowing will reduce them considerably. Maintaining a good vigorous sward by the methods outlined above is also recommended.

Pearlwort This prostrate forming plant has very slender stems and tiny bristle-like leaves. It can form dense, mossy looking mats which will respond to repeated treatment with 'Verdone' 2. Pearlwort is more common on the poorer soils on lawns kept mown too short. The best way of eliminating it is to feed the lawn and set the mower blades higher – about 2.5cm (1in) – plus the above mentioned treatment.

Yarrow This creeping plant has narrow leaves, deeply cut to resemble fern fronds in miniature. Large patches have a rich green mossy appearance. Left unmown, erect wiry stems grow up in summer, bearing flattened heads of tiny white or pinkish daisy flowers.

The comments under pearlwort mostly apply here also and a kill can sometimes be achieved with 'Verdone' 2, repeated several times during the season. Maintaining a vigorous sward of strong grass plants is essential to its final elimination so keep the grass growing well.

Moss Several species of moss are a natural constituent of grassland and it is neither possible nor particularly desirable to remove it entirely from a lawn. Indeed it is fair to say that too much attention is paid to methods of removal in most books on lawncraft. If a lawn is attended in the way described here, moss will present no problems.

For a quicker eradication, a proprietary moss killer, such as 'Lawnsman' Mosskiller, or lawn sand can be used at 120g per sq.m (4oz sq.yd). This can be done at any time of the year during dry weather, but autumn usually provides ideal conditions. The dead moss should be removed with a wire rake 10-14 days after the treatment.

Lawn daisy (above)

Moss (top right)

Speedwell (bottom right)

Lawn pests can cause damage by feeding on grass roots, thus weakening the turf, or by depositing earth on the surface so that it mars the appearance and makes mowing difficult. The following pests can be controlled with the right treatment.

Chafers Several kinds of chafer beetle have grubs which feed on roots, including those of grasses. Often known as white grubs, these pests are dirty white and fleshy, up to 3cm (1½in) or so in length but appearing smaller by always being curled to the shape of the letter C. They have a hard red-brown head and six legs just behind. Only rarely are they present in sufficient numbers to severely damage a lawn and then cause areas of wilting or dying grass. Soaking the affected area with a diluted solution of 'Sybol' will usually kill the grubs. One gallon of the solution will treat 12-16sq.m (15-20sq.yd). Preparations containing HCH, bromophos or diazinon will also be effective. This pest is unlikely to be a problem on a well maintained lawn.

Earthworms In general, earthworms have a beneficial effect on the fertility of the soil, but some species produce small digested soil heaps on the surface known as casts. These can be unsightly on an ornamental lawn of fine grasses and if in large quantities the worms may need controlling. Initially the casts should be swept or removed with a wire rake. If the condition quickly reappears, as it will do on the richer soils during moist weather, then apply a proprietary worm killer containing carbaryl or chlordane according to makers' instructions. Autumn is the best time to do this.

Leatherjackets These fat, leathery dirty-grey 2.5cm (1in) long worm-like pests are the larvae of the common crane-fly or 'flying daddy-long-legs'. They feed exclusively on grass roots and other grassland plants and occur in almost every lawn. When present in large numbers brown patches occur, particularly in dry weather.

The best method of control is 'Sybol' or HCH as mentioned under chafers. Bromophos or diazinon granules may also be effective. Alternatively, soak the lawn with water, preferably during the afternoon, and cover with sheets of black polythene.

There are two kinds of lawn pest: those that attack the roots from below and those that leave a deposit of earth on the surface. Leatherjackets (left) are root-eating pests that cause deterioration of the turf; earthworms (below) fall into the other category – they deposit wormcasts on the lawn surface making it uneven.

DISEASES

Lawn diseases are caused by fungal attacks, and these occur when the grass is not in good condition. Lack of food and water, bad drainage, compaction or mowing too close will allow disease to attack. Some of the more common diseases and their treatments are described here.

Dollar spot From late summer to early autumn, during mild wet spells, this fungus disease may strike, causing initially circular brown or bleached areas up to 5cm (2in) across. Later, if there are several of these, they spread and fuse together forming large irregular patches of dead grass. Another fungus disease causing similar damage is ophiobolus patch, which is more likely to occur in wet conditions on limy soil. Both diseases are difficult to control, but fortunately they are rare in lawns. The best cure is to cut out infected turf with at least 7.5-10cm (3-4in) all round, filling the hole with fresh soil and seed or a piece of turf.

Fairy rings Several fungi which live in grassland radiate from the point of infection like the spokes of a wheel, producing their fruiting bodies – toadstools – where the rim of the imaginary wheel would be. The fungus plant is in the form of white threads, known as hyphae, and lives by feeding on organic matter in the soil. Some fungi produce rings of extra lush grass next to rings of browning or dying grass. The dying grass is usually suffering from drought, caused by the dense growth of fungal hyphae which is waxy and prevents rain from reaching the roots. Later, as the fungus dies out behind the vigorously growing peripheral zone, it decays and releases valuable plant food, hence the rich green zone.

Not all fairy ring fungi produce the brownish zones, but even so the dark green rings may be considered unsightly. If so, then the following treatment can be tried.

Remove the ring of dark green grass plus a strip of turf 25-30cm (9-12in) wide on either side. Destroy the removed turf, preferably by burning. Fork the soil beneath to a depth of 25cm (9in), or deeper if the white hyphae can be seen below. Sterilize the infected soil with a product such as 'Clean-Up', making sure that the solution soaks down through the forked layer. Cover the treated area with a plastic sheet to intensify the action of the chemical; remove after 10 days. This is best carried out in summer when the soil is warm. After treatment, fill in and level the area and after a minimum period of eight weeks re-seed or turf the area. If the fairy ring is small or not very pronounced, then it is worthwhile spiking with a fork and watering with a 30g (1oz) solution of sulphate of iron to 10 litres (2½ gal) of water, using 4.6-7 litres (1-1½ gal) per square metre. This treatment may also be given to any area of the lawn where toadstool type fungi appear, although they seldom do any real damage to the grass.

Red thread This fungus trouble, also known as corticium disease, can occur at any time of the year, but is most prevalent in late summer and autumn. The fungal threads or hyphae grow amongst the foliage, creating a pinkish hue; later the leaves redden and then look

bleached. Red thread rarely forms patches larger than 15cm (6in) across and is only likely to appear on waterlogged lawns, particularly those also deficient in nitrogen. The disease will respond to treatment with Benlate + 'Activex'.

Snow mould Also known as Fusarium patch, this disease starts as small patches of yellow grass which gradually increase in size, browning in the middle later, the faintly pinkish cotton-like fungal growth mats the dying leaves together. It can occur at almost any time but mainly in autumn and winter. It does sometimes seem to follow a snow thaw, particularly where the snow was well trodden. Snow mould is fostered

Fairy rings are caused by parasitic fungi. The toadstools (above) can be cured easily, but the more damaging Marasmius oreades (top) prevents water from reaching grass roots.

by poor aeration and an over use of nitrogenous fertilizers, particularly when applied in autumn. Most of the proprietary turf fungicides, such as Benlate + 'Activex' will effect a cure. Very mild attacks may respond to sulphate of iron at 10g (¼oz) in 2 litre (½ gal) water per square metre.

THE LAWN YEAR

JANUARY

Note any areas where waterlogging occurs and persists and improve drainage. If the weather is mild and the soil not wet and sticky, aeration can still be carried out (see September entry). On moist soils, and particularly when snow has melted, watch out for snow mould disease.

FEBRUARY

The tasks for January may still be carried out in suitable weather. If worm casts are a nuisance, brush with a birch broom or scatter with a long cane held horizontally. Apply lawn sand for daisies, clover and moss, or a proprietary moss killer for the latter, at the end of the month.

MARCH

Aeration may still be carried out. Apply a dressing of 'Lawnsman' Lawn Feed, preferably after the first mowing which should be done once the new grass blades reach 6-7.5cm (2½-3in) in height. Seed sowing and turf laying can now take place. Towards the end of the month, a selective weedkiller can be used, as long as the grass is growing vigorously. Moss killers may be applied.

APRIL

Fertilizer may still be applied, preferably during showery weather, also moss killers and selective or hormone weedkillers. Sowing and turf laying may continue. Mow established lawns regularly.

MAY

Drought conditions are possible during this month, particularly in the south-east. Unless there are restrictions on water usage, begin watering the lawn to maintain vigorous healthy growth. If the grass still lacks vigour and a good, rich green appearance, apply 'Lawnsman' Lawn Feed or a dressing of sulphate of ammonia at 30g per sq.m (½oz sq.yd), watering in well unless a good rain follows. Apply weedkiller if and when necessary, or use 'Lawnsman' Weed and Feed.

JUNE

The May recommendations still apply. If the lawn is on a rapidly draining site, and dries out quickly, begin watering after 2-3 weeks have passed without rain. On the heavier soils being watering only 3-4 weeks after the last good rain.

JULY

All the comments for June still apply. Early in the month give a light feed. Scarify weed patches if they become a nuisance. Weedkillers may still be used if necessary. Mow regularly and water as necessary.

AUGUST

Towards the end of the month, particularly in the north, new lawns may be sown. During the same period, particularly if the month is cool, look out for dollar spot and red thread diseases and start worm control if this proves necessary.

SEPTEMBER

Towards the end of the month, aeration with a rake or hollow tined fork can be carried out. The comments on diseases and worm control still apply. This is the best month for sowing a lawn, providing the soil is neither too wet nor too dry. Towards the end of this month, work over the soil surface with a wire tined rake to aerate and remove moss. Small worn areas should be re-sown or turfed. If the grass lacks vigour, apply a fertilizer.

OCTOBER

Sowing can continue, providing the soil is not too wet, but this is the best month for turf laying, again providing soil conditions are suitable. If it is too dry, then watering must be carried out until rain arrives. Continue mowing all the time the grass is growing well. Aerating the soil with a wire tined rake or fork can still be done. Fertilizers, such as 'Lawnsman' Autumn Feed, may still be applied to established lawns during the first two weeks.

NOVEMBER

Turf laying may continue, but should be completed before the end of the month if possible. Unless the weather is very mild, the last mowing of the season should be by the end of the month. Aeration can still be carried out if soil conditions allow. Worm killers may still be applied.

DECEMBER

Aeration can still be carried out during mild, dry weather. Look out for dollar spot and red thread diseases.

INDEX AND ACKNOWLEDGEMENTS

Picture credits

Bernard Alfieri: 29, 45(b).
Ken Beckett: 38, 39(t), 40/1.
R. J. Corbin: 11(t,b), 12/3, 21, 24, 25, 26/7, 32(l,r), 34, 37, 45(t), 46/7.
John Glover: 1, 8, 16.

Iris Hardwick Library: 10, 17.
ICI: 6, 7(b), 39(b), 40, 41, 42, 43 (t,b).
Miki Slingsby: 4/5, 7(t), 9, 31.
Colin Watmough: 8/9.

Artwork by

Richard Prideaux & Steve Sandilands